A+ books

POLAR ANIMALS

CARIBOU

ARE AWESOME

by Jaclyn Jaycox

Consultant: Greg Breed
Associate Professor of Ecology
Institute of Arctic Biology
University of Alaska, Fairbanks

PEBBLE
a capstone imprint

A+ Books are published by Pebble,
1710 Roe Crest Drive, North Mankato, Minnesota 56003
www.mycapstone.com

Library of Congress Cataloging-in-Publication Data
Names: Jaycox, Jaclyn, 1983–author.
Title: Caribou Are Awesome / by Jaclyn Jaycox.
Description: North Mankato, Minnesota: an imprint of Pebble, [2020] |
    Series: A+. Polar Animals | Audience: Age 4–8. | Audience: K to Grade 3. |
    Includes bibliographical references and index.
Identifiers: LCCN 2018056708| ISBN 9781977108197 (hardcover) | ISBN
    9781977109996 (paperback) | ISBN 9781977108289 (ebook pdf)
Subjects: LCSH: Caribou—Juvenile literature. | Animals—Polar
    regions–Juvenile literature.
Classification: LCC QL737.U55 J39 2020 | DDC 599.65/8—dc23
LC record available at https://lccn.loc.gov/2018056708

Editorial Credits
Nikki Potts, editor; Kayla Rossow, designer; Morgan Walters, media researcher;
Laura Manthe, production specialist

Photo Credits
Alamy: Nature Picture Library, spread 10-11; iStockphoto: Athep, 21, Freder, top 15, Rumo, 12; Newscom: Sergey Gorshkov/Minden Pictures, 20; Shutterstock: Arildina, 23, critterbiz, top 24, David Boutin, 5, Dawn Wilson Photo, 27, Dinozzzaver, 26, Dmitry Chulov, 29, evgenii mitroshin, 14, Fufachew Ivan Andreevich, Cover, Jukka Jantunen, 22, longtaildog, 18, 28, Mara008, design element (blue), MarcinWojc, bottom 15, Menno Schaefer, 7, Mircea Costina, 9, Nadezhda Bolotina, top 17, Oliay, design element (ice window), photosoft, design element (ice), saulty72, 6, Scott E Read, bottom 24, Sergey Krasnoshchokov, spread 25-26, Sketchart, 8, Stefan Holm, 13, Terence Mendoza, 4, Tsuguliev, 19, Vladimir Melnikov, spread 16-17

Note to Parents, Teachers, and Librarians

This Polar Animals book uses full-color photographs and a nonfiction format to introduce the concept of caribou. *Caribou Are Awesome* is designed to be read aloud to a pre-reader or to be read independently by an early reader. Photographs help listeners and early readers understand the text and concepts discussed. The book encourages further learning by including the following sections: Table of Contents, Glossary, Read More, Internet Sites, Critical Thinking Questions, and Index. Early readers may need assistance using these features.

TABLE OF CONTENTS

Made for the Cold 4

Furry Caribou 6

Finding Food 14

Family Life 18

Staying Safe 24

Glossary 30

Read More 31

Internet Sites. 31

Critical Thinking Questions 32

Index 32

Made for the Cold

A cold wind blows across the icy tundra. *Brr!* Many animals cannot live in the Arctic. But caribou are found in areas with cold weather, ice, and snow.

Caribou are also called reindeer. They are part of the deer family.

Furry Caribou

Caribou are found in North America and Europe. They also live in Asia and Greenland. Most caribou spend winter in forests. They feed on moss.

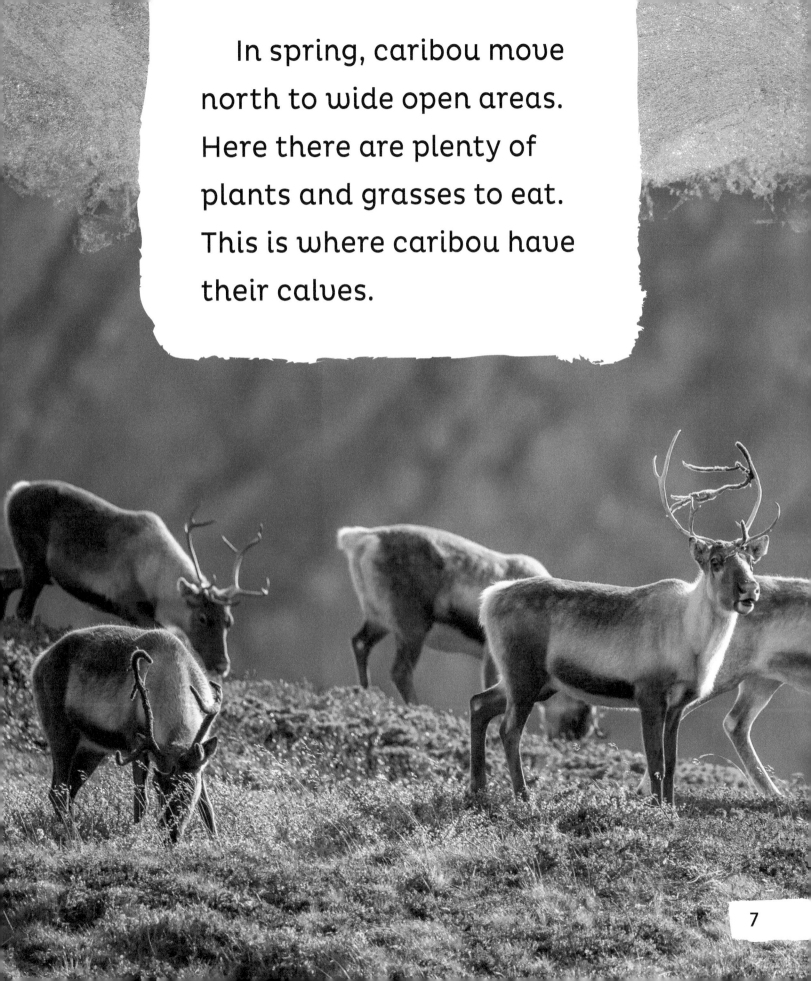

In spring, caribou move north to wide open areas. Here there are plenty of plants and grasses to eat. This is where caribou have their calves.

Caribou can be brown or white. They have two thick layers of fur. Their fur is very warm. Caribou are more likely to get too hot than to freeze.

A caribou's nose works like a heater. It warms up the air a caribou breathes in. This helps keep their bodies warm.

Caribou can be more than 5 feet (150 centimeters) tall. They can weigh more than 500 pounds (225 kilograms).

Both male and female caribou have antlers. Males use their antlers to fight with each other. Females use their antlers to protect their food. Antlers fall off and grow back every year.

Caribou have big hooves with fur on the bottom. The fur helps them walk on snow and ice without slipping. Caribou use their hooves to dig in snow. They also use their hooves to paddle when swimming.

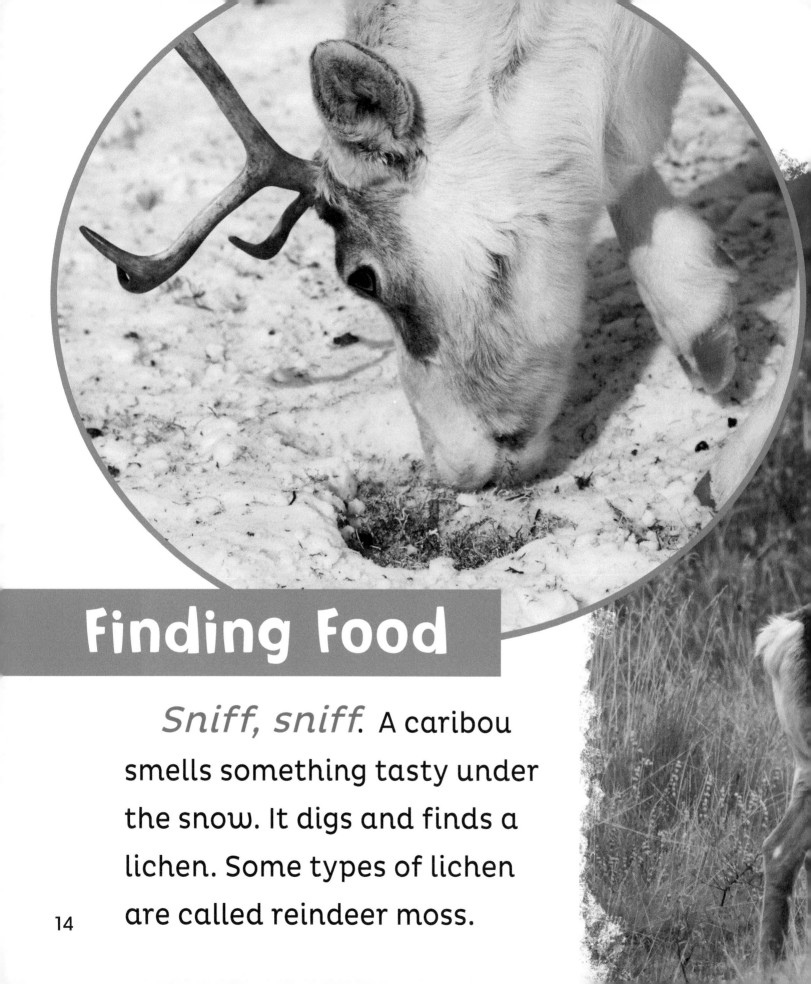

Finding Food

Sniff, sniff. A caribou smells something tasty under the snow. It digs and finds a lichen. Some types of lichen are called reindeer moss.

14

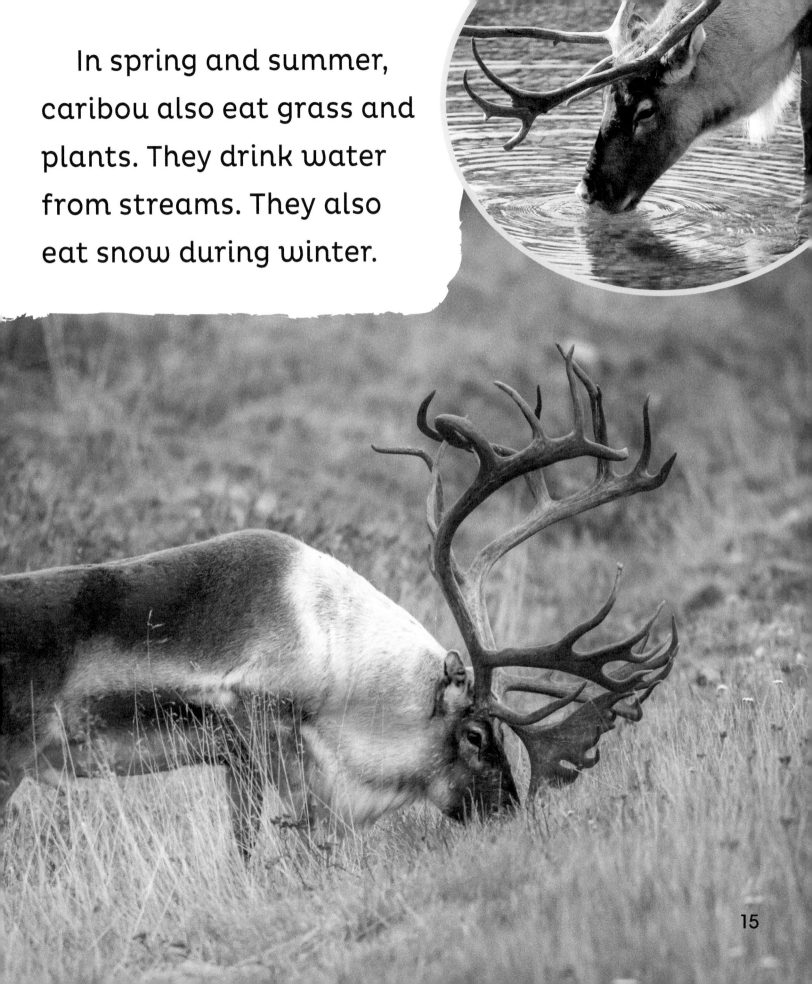

In spring and summer, caribou also eat grass and plants. They drink water from streams. They also eat snow during winter.

Caribou migrate in spring and fall. As many as 500,000 caribou move together. They travel up to 1,600 miles (2,575 kilometers) to look for food. In summer, a caribou can eat up to 12 pounds (5.4 kg) of food a day.

Family Life

Caribou live in herds. Some herds may only have 10 caribou. Others can have a few hundred. They communicate with each other using snorts and grunts.

When it's dark and snowy, it is hard for caribou to see. Their feet make clicking sounds when they walk. These sounds help the herd stay together.

Female caribou give birth to one calf in spring. Calves weigh about 9 pounds (4 kg). They are born with warm fur.

Calves can stand just minutes after being born. After a few hours, they can run faster than a human!

Calves grow very quickly. They drink milk from their mother for six months. The herd teaches calves how to stay safe.

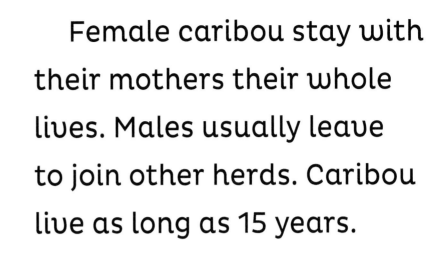

Female caribou stay with their mothers their whole lives. Males usually leave to join other herds. Caribou live as long as 15 years.

Staying Safe

Wolves and grizzly bears are caribous' biggest threat. Golden eagles try to snatch newborn caribou calves.

wolf

grizzly bear

The changing climate can harm caribou. The Arctic is getting warmer. There is more rain. When rain freezes, it traps caribous' food under ice. Caribou may not have enough to eat.

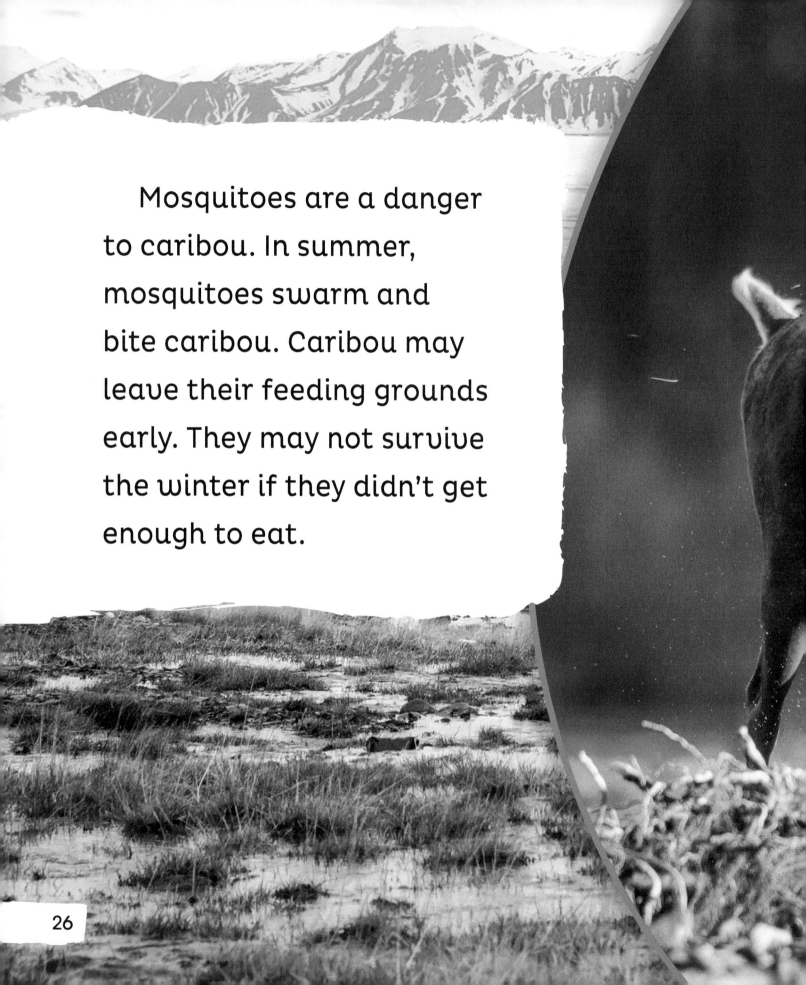

Mosquitoes are a danger to caribou. In summer, mosquitoes swarm and bite caribou. Caribou may leave their feeding grounds early. They may not survive the winter if they didn't get enough to eat.

There are about 5 million caribou in the world. Caribou eat, sleep, and travel together. They depend on each other.

Caribou help keep each other safe. These awesome polar animals are perfect for the Arctic!

GLOSSARY

antler (ANT-luhr)—large, branching, bony forms that grow on the heads of animals in the deer family

Arctic (ARK-tik)—the area near the North Pole; the Arctic is cold and covered with ice

climate (KLY-muht)—the average weather of a place throughout the year

herd (HURD)—a large group of animals that lives or moves together

hoof (HOOF)—the hard covering on an animal's foot

lichen (LYE-ken)—a flat, spongelike growth made of algae and fungi

migrate (MYE-grate)—to move from one place to another

mosquito (muh-SKEE-toh)—a small insect that bites animals and humans and sucks their blood

polar (POH-lur)—having to do with the icy regions around the North or South Pole

protect (pruh-TEKT)—to keep safe

swarm (SWORM)—to fly closely together, forming a dense mass

tundra (TUHN-druh)—a cold area where trees do not grow; the soil under the ground in the tundra is permanently frozen

READ MORE

Borgert-Spaniol, Megan. *Caribou*. North American Animals. Minneapolis: Bellwether Media, Inc., 2018.

Koestler-Grack, Rachel A. *Caribou*. North American Animals. Mankato, MN: Amicus, 2019.

Samuelson, Benjamin O. *Journey of the Caribou*. Massive Animal Migrations. New York: Gareth Stevens Publishing, 2018.

INTERNET SITES

National Geographic Kids, Caribou Profile
https://kids.nationalgeographic.com/animals/caribou/#caribou-standing-grass.jpg

Reindeer Facts for Kids
https://www.kidsplayandcreate.com/reindeer-facts-for-kids/

CRITICAL THINKING QUESTIONS

1. How do caribou stay warm?

2. Caribou eat mainly lichen. What is a lichen?
   (Hint: Use the glossary for help!)

3. What kinds of dangers do caribou face?

INDEX

antlers, 11

Arctic, 4, 25, 29

calves, 7, 20, 21, 22, 24

food, 6, 7, 11, 14, 15, 16, 22, 25, 26

fur, 8, 12, 20

herds, 18, 19, 23

hooves, 12

migration, 16

noses, 9

reindeer, 5

size, 10, 20

sounds, 18, 19

threats, 24, 25, 26

tundra, 4